NORMAN CASTLES

WILLIAM BUILDS CASTLES

William was crowned in Westminster Abbey on Christmas Day, 1066. He was not sure if the Saxon people would accept him as king.

Some of the crowd outside the Abbey started to shout and cheer. They meant to show that they welcomed William.

The Norman soldiers could not understand what the crowd was saying. They thought that the Saxons were rioting and so they attacked them. Many people were killed and houses burnt to the ground. It was not a good start.

William was worried by what had happened. Although a brave man, he was seen to tremble with fear. He determined to set up castles throughout England to protect the Normans.

The Normans had invented a way of building castles quickly. It was a bit like making sandcastles, but on a much bigger scale.

After digging a ditch, they raised a great mound in the middle. This was called a "motte" which is French for "mound".

On top of the mound they built a tower and surrounded it with a wooden fence. This was the strongest point of the castle.

Below the motte there was another enclosure surrounded by a fence. This was called the "bailey". The Normans built motte and bailey castles all over England.

To stop the Saxons from causing trouble, William introduced something called the "curfew". This meant that everybody had to put their fires out at eight o'clock and go to bed.

It needed more than a curfew, however, to keep England peaceful. In 1069 there was a great rebellion in the north of England. William defeated the rebels and treated them cruelly.

A year later, Hereward the Wake led another revolt against the Normans in the east of England. His base was in the Fenland marshes. It was a long time before William could find Hereward and defeat him.

The Normans were still not safe, and they began to build bigger and stronger castles made out of stone. Stone walls were harder to knock down than wooden walls and could not be set on fire.

This is the original Tower of London. It was started by William the Conqueror and completed by his son, William Rufus. The picture shows how it looked when it was first built.

A CASTLE UNDER SIEGE

For many years after William's reign, the new Norman kings had to keep order amongst their subjects. This picture shows a castle belonging to a later Norman baron who has rebelled against the king. With his knights, the king is seen deciding how to capture the castle. The king asks some questions.

These are the king's questions

1. How can we cross the moat? It is 5 metres deep and 30 metres wide. Our men cannot swim wearing armour.

2. When we are across the moat how can we break through the outer wall?

3. There are archers in the righthand corner tower who can shoot at us as we break through the wall. How can we destroy the tower?

4. When we are through the wall we shall be able to let our troops in through the castle entrance. How can we lower the drawbridge?

5. How can we protect our troops from stones and arrows shot from the castle walls?

6. How can we make the defenders tired and discouraged before we make our main attack?

7. When we launch our main attack on the walls we must prevent the defenders from collecting all their men together to fight us at one place. How can we do that?

8. When we break through the outer wall we shall be in the bailey but will still have to attack the keep—the strongest part of the castle. What difficulties shall we meet?

ADVICE FOR THE KING

Did you have the same solutions?

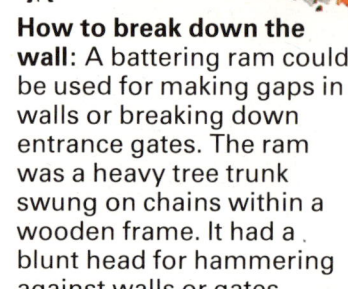

How to get across the moat: The moat could be filled with earth and rubble. A "tortoise", which was a defence device on wheels, could be used to protect the soldiers from arrows and stones whilst they were working.

How to destroy a tower: A tunnel could be dug up to and under the tower to undermine it. Strong wooden props would support the heavy masonry. These were set on fire so that they would collapse the tower above.

How to break down the wall: A battering ram could be used for making gaps in walls or breaking down entrance gates. The ram was a heavy tree trunk swung on chains within a wooden frame. It had a blunt head for hammering against walls or gates.

How to lower the drawbridge: In early Norman castles the bridges over moats were "withdraw" bridges. They were pulled back as shown above. Gatehouses were, however, well defended and a strong party of men would be needed to capture it.

5

How to protect the troops: Heavy wooden shields called "mantlets" could be used to give shelter to the archers whilst the wall was being broken down. They were probably made of several layers of wood, leather and other light material.

6

How to discourage and tire the defenders: Siege engines could be used to fire heavy stones into the castle to kill people and destroy buildings. This is a mangonel. The throwing arm was powered by twisted ropes. On page 16, a model of another siege engine, a trebuchet, is explained. It is a working model.

7

How to prevent the defenders from collecting together in one place: Scaling ladders could be used to climb the walls, and tall towers on wheels, called "belfroys", could be built. With these, several attacks could be made at different points at the same time to divide the defence.

8

Difficulties to be met inside the keep: Drawbridges would be removed from gaps in the entrance passages from the forebuilding; spiral staircases in castles always wound to the right going upwards. This favoured the defenders for the attackers' sword hands were obstructed by the central pillar.

9

Problem picture

Guests have arrived at a Norman castle. Food is being brought to them in the great hall. Study the picture and see if you can solve these problems:

1. One of the servants is carrying a log of wood. What is it for?

2. The servant on the left carries a bowl and towel. What are these for?

3. There is a tall wooden board standing beside the window. What is it for?

4. One of the visitors has thrown a meat bone on the floor for his dog. Will it spoil the carpet?

5. It is early evening, can you see how the hall was lit?

6. Why are dogs allowed into the hall during a meal?

7. There are no plates on the table. How will the food be served to guests?

8. One of the servants is carrying meat on sticks. Why is this?

DID YOU SOLVE THESE PROBLEMS?

The log is for the fire. There were fireplaces in the walls of castle keeps where big logs were burned. Chimneys did not go to the roof but through the great thicknesses of outside walls.

The bowl and the towel were for guests to wash their hands before eating. They ate with their fingers and shared the same dishes of food so that clean fingers were very important.

The board by the window is a shutter. This would be put into place in the window at night to keep out the cold—or during the day in winter—for there was no glass for windows in early castles.

There is no carpet on the floor. Rushes were cut from pond or river banks and strewn on the floor. When they became dirty, they were gathered up, burned, and fresh rushes laid.

At dusk, candles were put on tables and the torches fixed to wall brackets were lit. Both made lots of smoke but gave very little light. People went to bed early in winter.

The Normans were very fond of dogs. They kept them for hunting—to search out game. Dogs were treated as pets between hunts. Greyhounds, staghounds and boarhounds were their favourites.

The sticks with meat skewered on them were small spits. There were no cooking stoves so food had to be either boiled in a cauldron or roasted on spits.

Only the lord and lady and their chief guests might have silver plates for their food. Everybody else had a large slice of bread called a "trencher" upon which they placed each course of the meal. When they had finished eating the trenchers were collected and given to the poor—or the dogs.

13

TREBUCHET—A WORKING MODEL

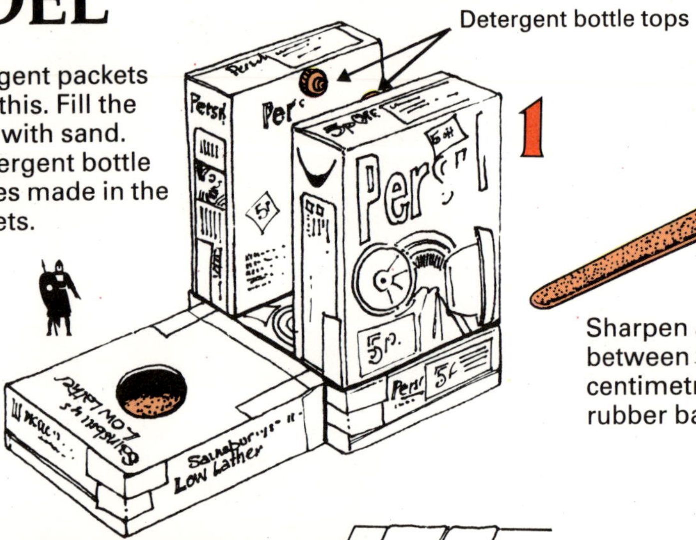

Fit four detergent packets together like this. Fill the bottom ones with sand. Glue two detergent bottle tops into holes made in the upright packets.

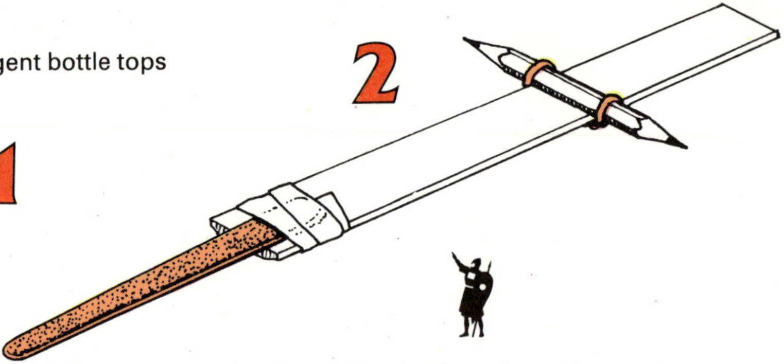

Detergent bottle tops

Sharpen a stub of pencil at both ends to fit exactly between the bottle tops. Tape an emery board of about 18 centimetres to a ruler. Fix them to the pencil stub—use a rubber band. This is the arm of the trebuchet.

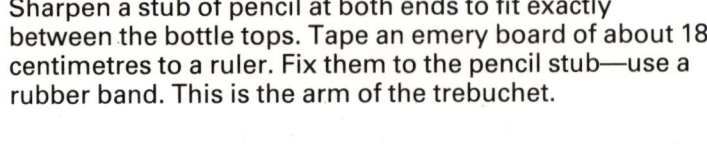

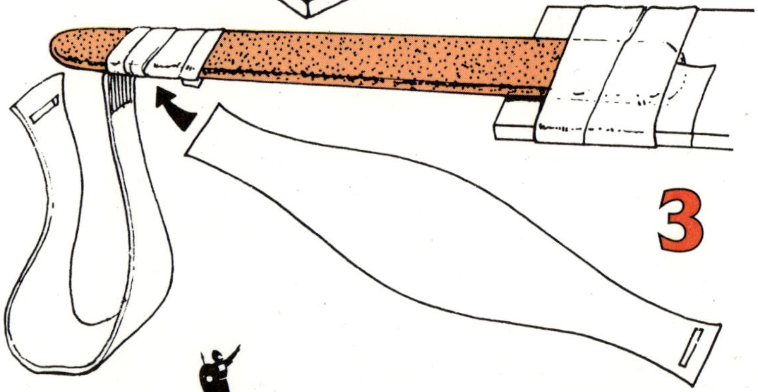

Cut a sling from a strip from a plastic carrier bag. Shape it like this and tape one end to the emery board.

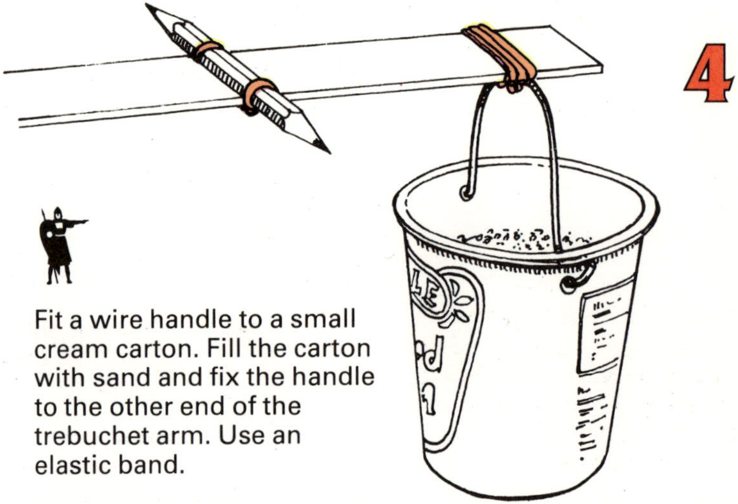

Fit a wire handle to a small cream carton. Fill the carton with sand and fix the handle to the other end of the trebuchet arm. Use an elastic band.

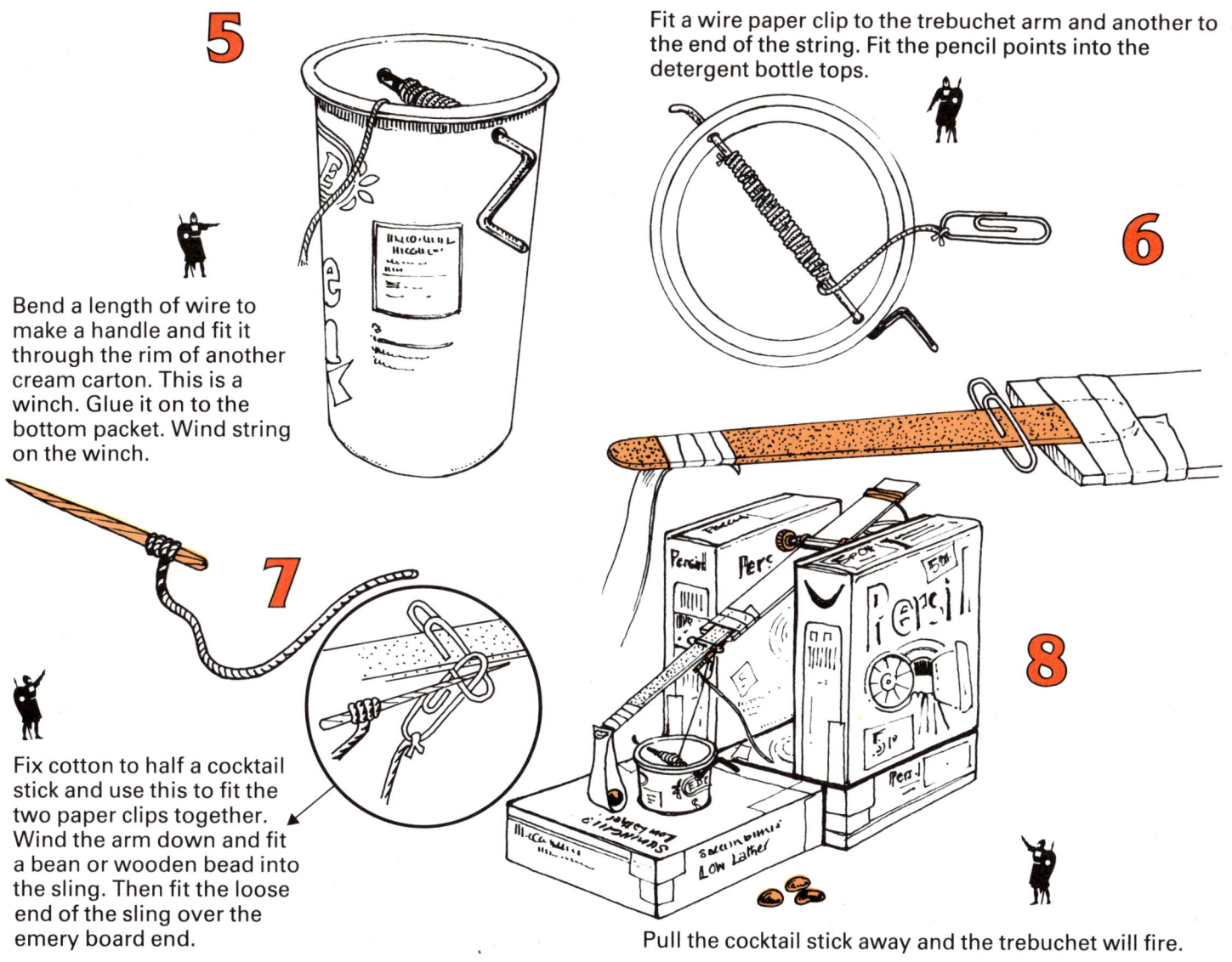

5

6 Fit a wire paper clip to the trebuchet arm and another to the end of the string. Fit the pencil points into the detergent bottle tops.

Bend a length of wire to make a handle and fit it through the rim of another cream carton. This is a winch. Glue it on to the bottom packet. Wind string on the winch.

7 Fix cotton to half a cocktail stick and use this to fit the two paper clips together. Wind the arm down and fit a bean or wooden bead into the sling. Then fit the loose end of the sling over the emery board end.

8 Pull the cocktail stick away and the trebuchet will fire.

15

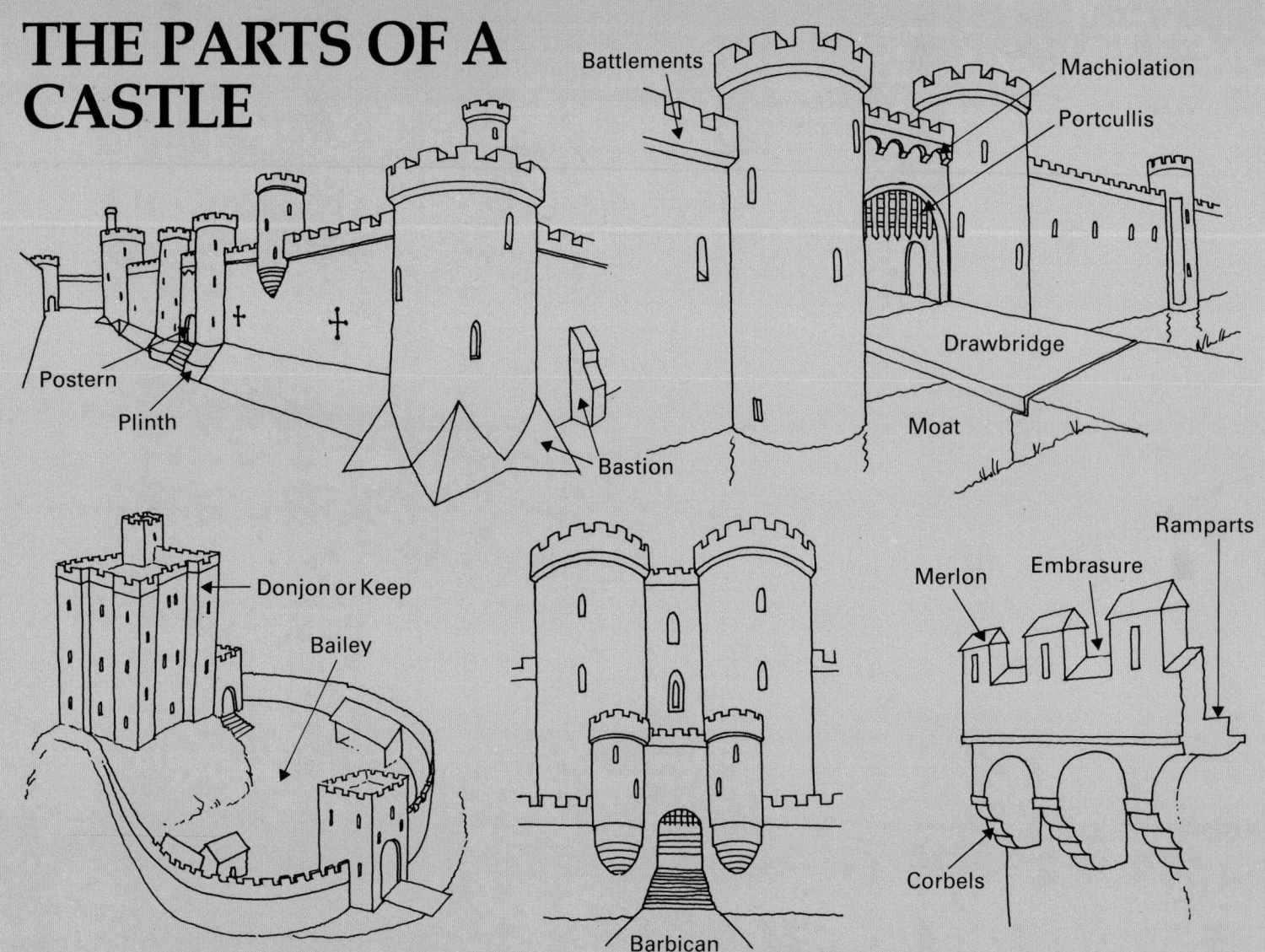